COOL ANIMALS

Kids Coloring Book

Get excited with this unique and cool coloring book for children and you will be amazed! This well designed color book was inspired by curiosity of children who ask questions about animals. There are 38 different pictures capturing fun activities performed by animals that are imaginative. And the uniqueness of this coloring book is that each of the animals is wearing a pair of sunglasses.

Whether it is showing cat fishing, rhino driving, or describing giraffe typing and frog reading, not only the children but also the adults would enjoy browsing through the pages and be fascinated to find out what's on the next page. When kids start coloring, they might start wondering how to play soccer, what do computers do, or can they go skiing like the penguin does. While they are having fun coloring the animals, they will also learn more about arts, sports, nature and cognitive skills.

Do not hesitate and order it today, and your kids would love it!

Any question or suggestion is welcome!
brothertuzi@gmail.com

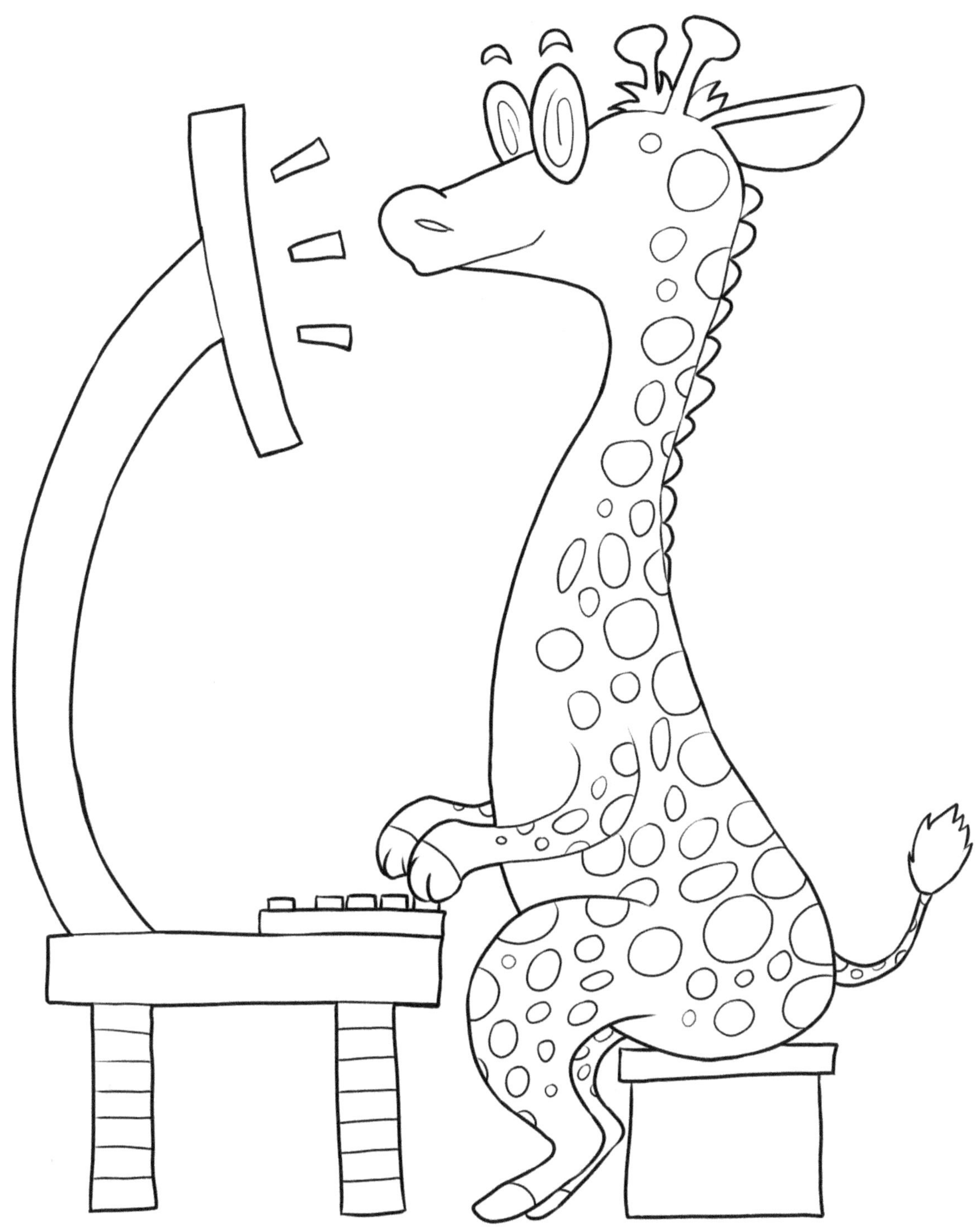

OK

ABC